Haiti
my country

Rogé thanks Julie Boisvert for her inspiring photographs and Clarel Legouté for his lovely smile!

English translation copyright © 2014, Fifth House Publishers
Originally published as *Haïti mon pays*: © 2010, Éditions de la Bagnole

Published in Canada by Fifth House Publishers,
195 Allstate Parkway, Markham, Ontario L3R 4T8

Published in the United States by Fifth House Publishers,
311 Washington Street, Brighton, Massachusetts 02135

10 9 8 7 6 5 4 3 2 1

Library and Archives Canada Cataloguing in Publication
Haiti my country
ISBN 978-1-92708-323-9 (Paperback)
Data available on file

Publisher Cataloging-in-Publication Data (U.S.)
Haiti my country
ISBN 978-1-92708-323-9 (Paperback)
Data available on file

Fifth House Publishers acknowledges with thanks the Canada Council for the Arts, and the Ontario Arts Council for their support of our publishing program. We acknowledge the financial support of the Government of Canada through the Canada Book Fund (CBF) for our publishing activities.

Cover and interior design by Tanya Montini
Cover image by Rogé
Printed in China by Sheck Wah Tong Printing Press Ltd.

Haiti
my country

Poems by Haitian Schoolchildren
Illustrated by Rogé
Translated by Solange Messier

FIFTH
HOUSE

Faces and Landscapes

When introduced to a poem, I do not like to know the age of the poet. With a novel, I always end up knowing the approximate age of the author. I only have to read attentively to revisit the era he or she grew up in (through a song, a place, an obsolete expression, or a particular event).

A poet often evokes the glory of nature, for no other reason than for the pure joy of it. For a novelist, nature is often seen through the eyes of the main character – during a car ride or on a long walk with a lover, for instance. Nature might also be used to express the wretchedness of a broken heart, or the sudden, glowing joy of a carefree child starting out on life's journey. The young poets whose work you will read have placed their easels in the middle of landscapes. Clearly, nature is their primary subject. Their ways of describing it remind me of primitive painters. From their pens flow such elegant scenes that we tend to wonder if they reflect the reality of Haiti.

After the ongoing deforestation of the last few decades came a succession of cyclones, deadly floods, and then the horrific earthquake. I should clarify that these poems were written before the earthquake of January 12, 2010. What's more, the region where these young poets live has been largely unaffected by the calamities that I have just mentioned. The natural landscapes that surround these teenagers inspire such dreams that visitors are often surprised they originated in Haiti. Ricardo Jocelyn lifts his head toward "an azure sky scattered with small white clouds." And Lordanie Théodore, while strolling, breathes in a "loving scent." We're at the heart of Southwest Haiti, a region that I am unfamiliar with because, for some mysterious reason, I have never been there. I'm here now to view the region through the eyes of the young poets. Nevertheless, Petit-Goâve, where I grew up, isn't as far from the south as I had believed. And my adolescence is not too different from those of these young dreamers. I feel, like they do, the secret joy one feels about living near such charming vistas. We might prefer to keep our emotions private, but they are so powerful that they seem to seep through our pores.

I observe Marie-Andrèle who is so fascinated by the "yellow mango" that she sings to it, hoping for it to fall: "Balance yourself below the branch." And I remember, like Marie-France Étienne, the "heavy rains" in June "and the giant noon sun." Everything is seen in vivid colour, reminiscent of a tropical Matisse painting: a red mango, a green window, with some purple here and there. What a celebration! And almost impossibly, it distracts us from the devastation caused by the earthquake. Such energy inhabits these adolescents! It overflows and consoles us, even as unfathomable sadness invades our hearts. Their vitality is irresistible. But as heavenly as the setting is, it does not distract them from the human condition. They are not fools.

Even though I'm disinterested in knowing the age of these poets, I do love to see the faces of those who speak to me. I do not know if the illustrations are true likenesses of the young writers, but I love the portraits that accompany the verses because they blend with the landscape and give us the true face of the country – a snapshot of its future. It is not common to see such sober faces in Haiti, where we still believe we must accentuate our zest for life and add some colour. The illustrator (I say illustrator and not painter because these portraits force us to think rather than to look) seems to be trying to resolve a deep mystery behind the faces that are suddenly unreadable.

Why is that? Perhaps it's because they suggest a peaceful, even idyllic world, when we know that terrible turmoil advances toward them. That's what makes them so poignant. The desert, gaining ground, threatens this harmonious world. Misery gallops toward these young men and women, who are presently filled with laughter. Here they stand so confident of their future. Judes-Roldes Raymond even has time to slip us her love of flowers, "especially pink flowers," before melding with the landscape. And to ensure that no one sends her a bouquet, she points out that she prefers them "attached to their roots." How much time will it take before these young faces are carried away by time? Who will be left to evoke such joy on this bereft island? Other young people, of course. Because in Haiti, poets grow as fast as the trees.

Dany Laferrière

TO MY FAMILY,

Rogé

I want to make it radiate everywhere
To make it known that Haiti is a gift from the heavens
Witnessing its greenery, its palm,
Apricot, mango, and avocado trees

The breeze caressing them as they dance
Their ripe fruit perched on high
Reminds one of the Genesis...
These oranges more sweet than sugar
More flavourful than honey

Each day in which the sun rises
Illuminating hills and rivers provides comfort for our worries

Upon awakening we hear the song of our neighbour's rooster
A beautiful concert to the ears of the merchants
Parading the streets of my country

Oh, Haiti! How beautiful you are in my eyes!
We come from everywhere, from all around you, to contemplate

Not far from your eternal and pure white beaches
We can smell your loving scent, intoxicating your people
Who sing for you, Haitian nature...

Lordanie Théodore

I dream

Of millions of flying birds
Around a tiny island without shelter, without shade
Hail and rain invade its sheet metal
Large trees inhibit its land from plummeting
From south to north
I walk in a garden of gold
By crossing wooded mountains
To Calcaneum
After each night of marvel
The citizens awaken under a sun
That protects the beaches from the cold sea
My gaze stops on a beach
Filled with people and belongings
Children who play, who chat
There, so jealous, rebellious
Begin to sing nonstop
Suddenly, I awaken
While imagining that it was all real
I open wide my eyes and ears
I look through the window
It's completely the opposite

I do not want to see these things in dreams
But in reality...

Jean-Pierre Paul Durand

At the peasant's garden
Everything is flourishing
Everything is goat pepper, hot pepper
Everything is red pea, black pea
Everything is sweet potato
Everything is fresh
At the peasant's garden

At the peasant's garden
Everything is Tonm-Tonm
Everything is green landscape, green scenery
Everything is cassava
Everything is callaloo
Everything is edible
At the peasant's garden

At the peasant's garden
Everything is millet
Everything is varieties of yam, various tastes
Everything is watercress
Everything is malanga
Everything is food
At the peasant's garden

Aldaïne Louis

Little home
Of wood or concrete
Of sheet metal or straw
Surrounded by flowers and green trees
Welcomes children
Receives parents
After a day of hard labour
Protects family
From heavy rains
And the giant noon sun
When all of a sudden clouds arrive
To travel the sky while singing a beautiful song
Come rain, come rain
Cool off the sheet metal
Of my little home!

Marie-France Étienne

In the countryside
We see a thatched cottage made of straw and earth
Small shelter for humble people
Happy to live on their ancestors' land
Little house of stone
Where the fresh air of unspoiled nature breathes
Bordered by garden and flowers
By banana trees, mango trees
That give us good fruit
Little house of thatch
Of sheet metal, brick, or rock that represents
So much for the family reuniting at night
Telling tales of our history
Past and present...

Dismy Borgela

Ripe mango
Fresh mango
Yellow mango
Mango in-between
Mango clusters
Balance yourself below the branch
Produce more mangos
That taste of honey and delight
For the lovers of the universe
All while preparing your supply of light

Marie-Andrèle Charlot

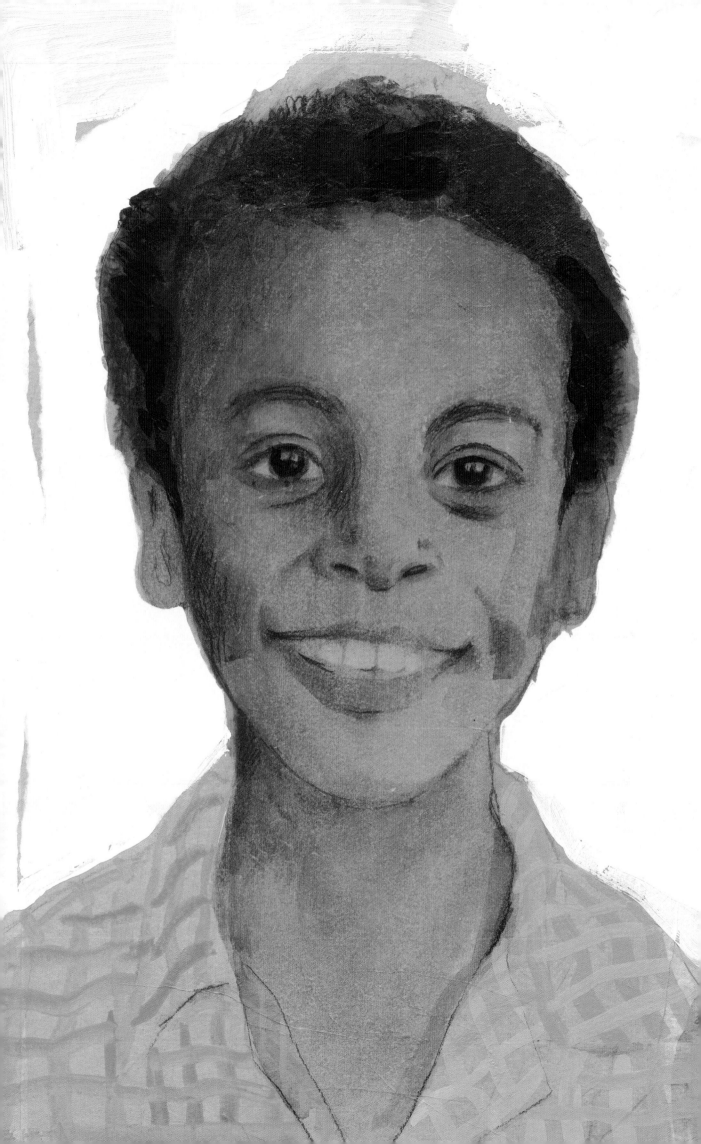

Everyone is fine in this rustic setting
Where we can lie out in the shade of the coconut trees
Savouring the pleasures of the golden fruit on the mango trees
Away from politics

From the azure sky scattered with small white clouds
Arises the morning sun
There, where no evil exists
We live peacefully

That's where we find genuine life
Where we breathe in clean air
Where cabins surrounded by beautiful greenery
Embellish the multicoloured flowers

Ricardo Jocelyn

Hibiscus bush of my country
Bordering the roads of my town
You charm my friends with your flowers, red, pink, and fancy yellow
You brighten up my yard and my fence
With your lovely multicoloured buds
Passersby look at you and smile
I love you, too
For the pretty colours with which you honour my home
Making me very proud
And I am happy to sit beside you
On the grass in my yard
I watch you with joy
Sometimes I smile at you as the sun rises
I especially adore living near you,
Hibiscus, because you are my favourite flower!

Dealine Dorcy

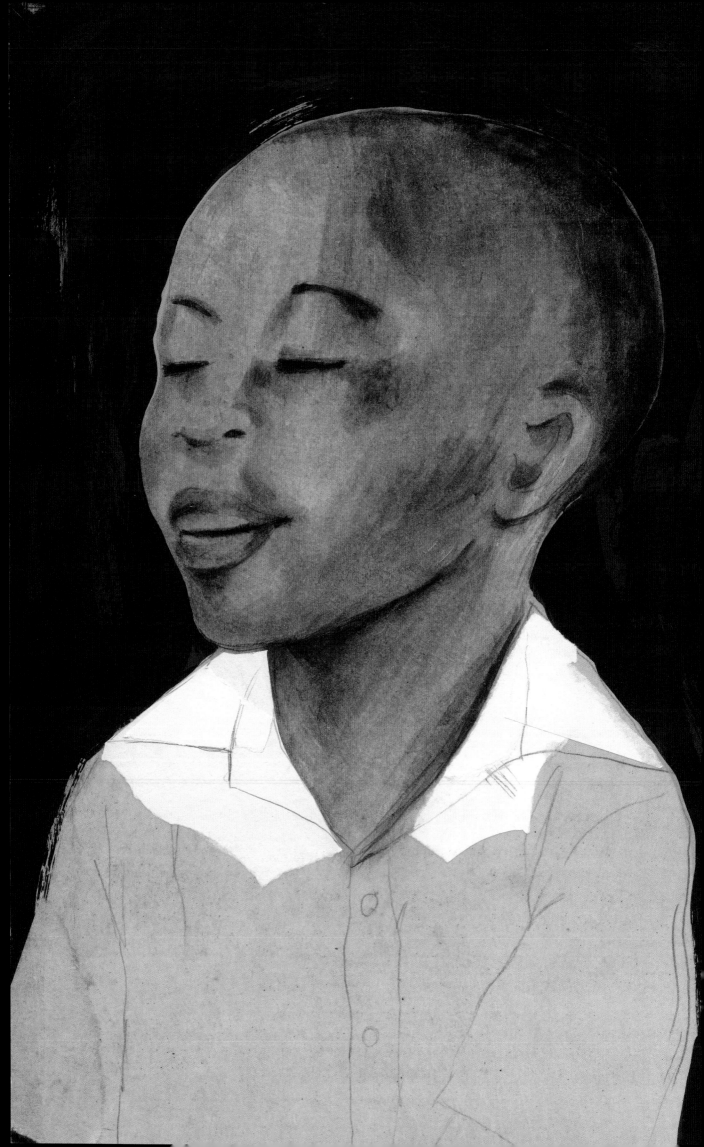

Haiti! A beautiful land that the warm sun illuminates,
appears extraordinary in the eyes of children
because of the songs of lively birds
amongst its fragrant flowers.

In this beautiful setting stretches dazzling greenery
where we find small curved houses,
flourishing mango trees at the end of lanes,
and ripening oranges.

Along the paths, peasants come from the market
carrying baskets of produce on their heads.

Their children wait for their return home, for surprises to share,
and to swim after the feast in the river just around the bend.

Everything is born, everything lives, and everything perishes.
But this country, her exceptional natural beauty—
I want her to live forever.

Judson Éliona

Humble little huts
That decorate the countryside
Where our companions live
Made only of clay and straw
Invite us to take shelter under their shade
To enjoy the natural cool
And relieve us from extreme heat

Madième Thercidor

The pretty flowers of my country are to me
Like pink butterflies
That smile at the sun.
I especially like pink flowers! The pink ones!
The charming pink flowers in my garden
Of multicoloured flowers:
Yellow, green, pink, red.
They are all lovely
Attached to their roots.
The giant sun shines in the sky
To the delight of the red flowers
In my garden.

Judes-Roldes Raymond

Magnificent country becomes
Broken land
All smiles are lost

Annie Hum

When we have a day
Of thousands of sacrifices in a country of tears,
People come here to rebuild their thoughts
Between the sea, the beach, the mountains, and the sky.

On the distant horizon, the sun disappears
To refresh our souls.
We observe the sea and the sky
In harmony, awakening tenderness within us.

While looking up to the mountains
They become neighbours to the sky
That carry the banner of our hope
Into another tomorrow, another sunrise.

Angelo Borgela

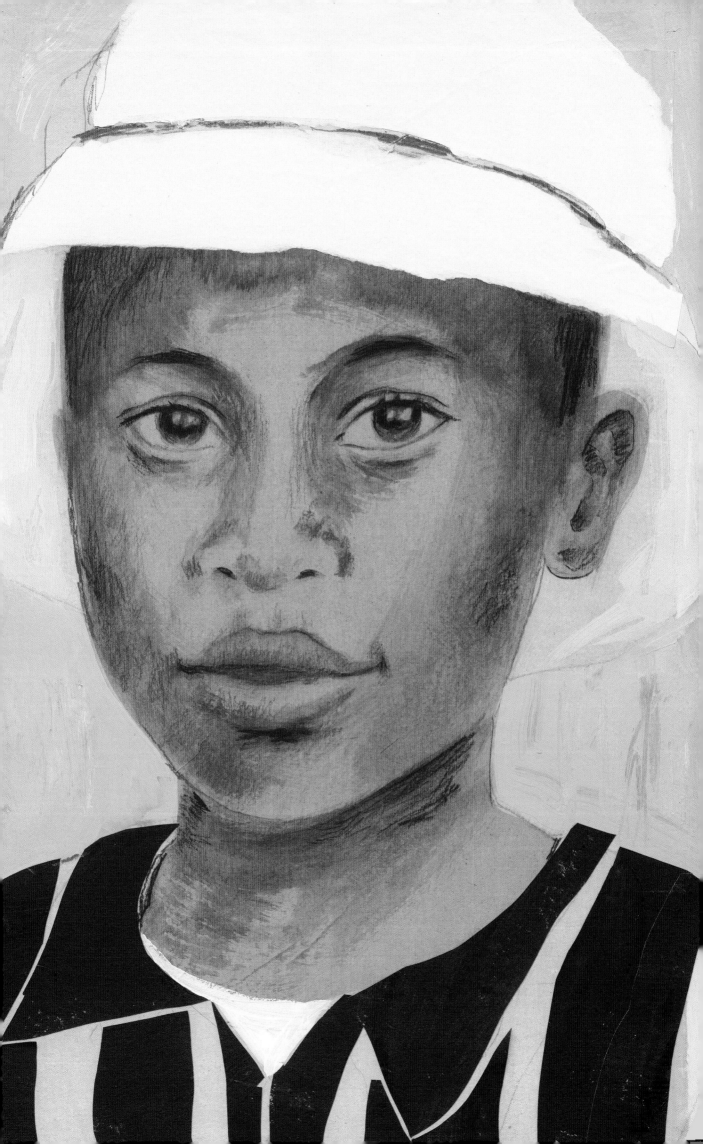

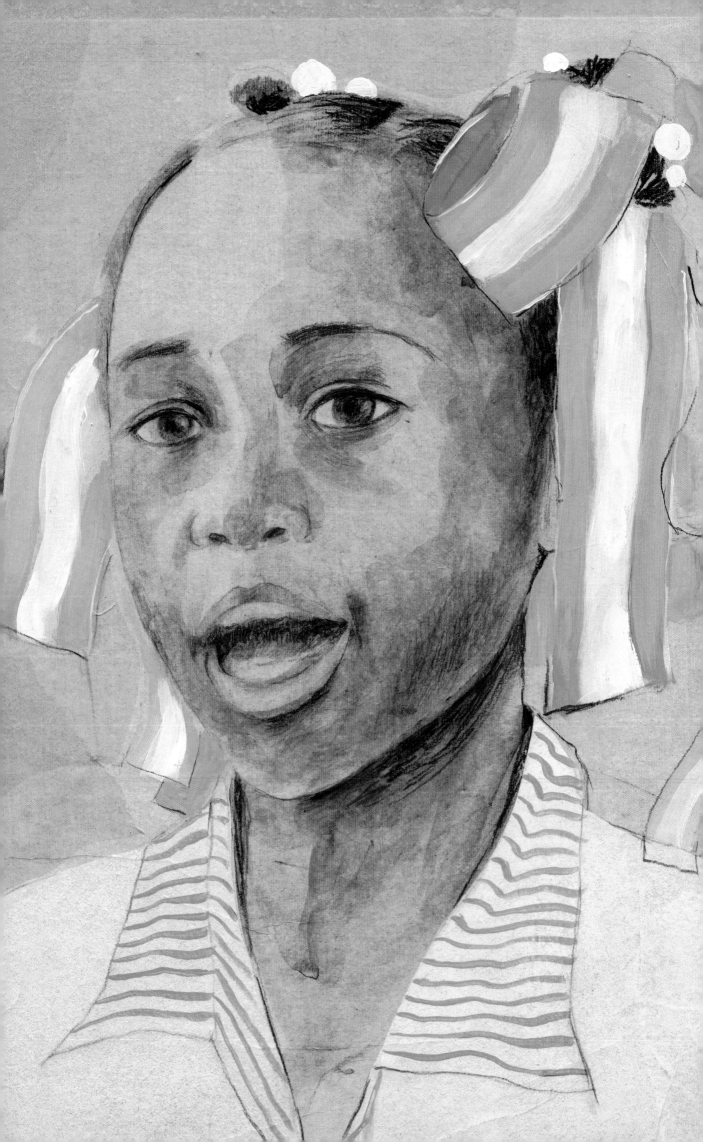

Haitian trees
Always dancing
For the wind that caresses them
Is a source of survival for us
From the mango tree to the coconut tree
From the soursop tree to the pomegranate tree
From the papaya tree to the avocado tree
From fruit to foliage
Food for the poor

Haitian trees
Always growing
Benefiting solely from nature
Their shade for relaxation
Their shelter for the sky's birds

Haitian trees
Always hoping
Through the goodness of life
Help to construct houses and furniture
Are necessary to create charcoal (alas!)
All, from the Haitian mahogany to giant oak
From the immense pine in the forest to calabash
To the cacao tree
All offer hope and life to all of us
We must take care of them

Jeanne Dadley Zamor

I love...
A flower, a fruit, a cottage, a man
A multitude of things
The colour purple
A small house of straw
A red bird on my roof
A flamboyant
Mauve-yellow, red-pink blossom
One flower, a bouquet of flowers
A green fig
A green window
A thatched cottage of stone
A red mango, another green
An adorned, verdant countryside
A living root
A better life
A country

Janaïe Orgella

What remains of you…

the unexpected chance to see
that the day finally breaks, and turns into night
for the better, and for the joy of reconciliation
heaven and earth, water of life, and luxuriant nature
to satisfy, to gratify
by the sweat of his brow
the need to build himself

whiteness and greenery
accompanied the day
the freshwater wedding

PERPÉTUE SULNEY

Perpétue Sulney, a teacher, represents the Foundation du Renouveau Pédagogique de Camp-Perrir (FRPCP), a non-profit organization that promotes and nurtures the rebirth of the science of education at Camp-Perrin (a small village in the southern Republic of Haiti).

Lordanie Théodore, born in 1994

Jean-Pierre Paul Durand, born in 1993

Aldaïne Louis, born in 1995

Marie-France Étienne, born in 1995

Dismy Borgela, born in 1995

Marie-Andrèle Charlot, born in 1997

Ricardo Jocelyn, born in 1991

Derline Dorcy, born in 1996

Judson Éliona, born in 1993

Madième Thercidor, born in 1996

Judes-Roldes Raymond, born in 1996

Annie Hum, born in 1999

Angelo Borgela, born in 1991

Jeanne Dadley Zamor, born in 1996

Janaïe Orgella, born in 1995